PENGUIN BOOKS

ON DEATH

Timothy Keller started Redeemer Presbyterian Church in New York City with his wife, Kathy, and their three sons. Redeemer grew to nearly 5,500 regular Sunday attendees and helped to start more than three hundred new churches around the world. In 2017 Keller moved from his role as senior minister at Redeemer to the staff of Redeemer City to City, an organization that helps national church leaders around the world reach and minister in global cities. He is the author of *The Prodigal Prophet*, *God's Wisdom for Navigating Life*, as well as *The Meaning of Marriage*, *The Prodigal God*, and *The Reason for God*, among others.

ALSO BY TIMOTHY KELLER

The Reason for God

The Prodigal God

Counterfeit Gods

Generous Justice

Jesus the King

Center Church

Every Good Endeavor

Walking with God Through Pain and Suffering

Encounters with Jesus

Prayer

Preaching

Making Sense of God

Hidden Christmas

Rediscovering Jonah (previously published as
The Prodigal Prophet)

On Birth

Hope in Times of Fear

WITH KATHY KELLER

The Meaning of Marriage

The Songs of Jesus

God's Wisdom for Navigating Life

The Meaning of Marriage: A Couple's Devotional

On Marriage

On Death

TIMOTHY
KELLER

PENGUIN BOOKS

PENGUIN BOOKS
An imprint of Penguin Random House LLC
penguinrandomhouse.com

All Bible references are from the New International Version
(NIV), unless otherwise noted.

ISBN 9780143135371 (paperback)
ISBN 9780525507031 (ebook)

Printed in the United States of America
2nd Printing

Set in Adobe Garamond Pro with Neutraface
Designed by Sabrina Bowers

Contents

Introduction to the How to Find God Series

Life is a journey, and finding and knowing God is fundamental to that journey. When a new child is born, when we approach marriage, and when we find ourselves facing death—either in old age or much earlier—it tends to concentrate the mind. We shake ourselves temporarily free from absorption in the whirl of daily life and ask the big questions of the ages:

Am I living for things that matter?

Will I have what it takes to face this new stage of life?

Do I have a real relationship with God?

The most fundamental transition any human being can make is what the Bible refers to as the new birth (John 3:1–8), or becoming a "new creation" (2 Corinthians 5:17). This can happen at any time in a life, of course, but often the circumstances that lead us to vital faith in Christ occur during these tectonic shifts in life stages. Over forty-five years of ministry, my wife, Kathy, and I have seen that people are particularly open to exploring a relationship with God at times of major life transition.

In this series of short books we want to help readers facing major life changes to think about what constitutes the truly changed life. Our purpose is to give readers the Christian foundations for life's most important and profound moments. We start with birth and baptism, move into marriage, and conclude with death. Our hope is that these slim books will provide guidance, comfort, wisdom, and, above all, will help point the way to finding and knowing God all throughout your life.

Foreword

As we age, Tim and I find ourselves encountering death, both pastorally and personally, more and more often. Our closest friends and family are now beginning to die. Over the last eighteen months, we have had three deaths in our family; in just the past three months we have talked to both a friend and a family member about how to face their impending deaths. Much of what we say in those conversations is in this book.

The foundation of *On Death* is a sermon preached by my husband at my sister Terry Hall's funeral on January 6, 2018. She died on Christmas Day, at home, surrounded by family after a lengthy struggle with metastatic breast cancer. She knew she was dying and spent time leaving instructions for us on the hymns, prayers, and other elements she wanted for her funeral service. She was adamant that Tim should preach the Gospel at her funeral and not merely talk about her life (as much as we loved and admired her). She knew that "death tends to concentrate the mind wonderfully"[1] and she wanted those present at her funeral to be prepared for their own deaths.

This book is dedicated to her, and to her husband, Bob, and daughters, Ruth Hall Ramsey and Rachael Hall. The sermon that day was, by all accounts, moving and memorable. The request to have it published came from her sisters, Sue and Lynn, and her brother, Steve.

KATHY KELLER
JULY 2018

On Death

The Fear
of Death

Conscience Makes Cowards of Us All

. . . that by his death he might break the power of him who holds the power of death—that is, the devil—and free those who all their lives were held in slavery by their fear of death.

—HEBREWS 2:14-15

D eath is the Great Interruption, tearing loved ones away from us, or us from them.

Death is the Great Schism, ripping apart the material and immaterial parts of our being and sundering a whole person, who was never meant to be disembodied, even for a moment.

Death is the Great Insult, because it reminds us, as Shakespeare said, that we are worm food.[1]

> [We are] literally split in two: [Man] has an awareness of his own splendid uniqueness in that he sticks out of nature with a towering majesty, and yet he goes back into the ground a few feet in order to blindly and dumbly rot and disappear forever.[2]

Death is hideous and frightening and cruel and unusual. It is not the way life is supposed to be, and our grief in the face of death acknowledges that.

Death is our Great Enemy, more than anything. It makes a claim on each and every one of us, pursuing us relentlessly through all our days. Modern people write and talk endlessly about love, especially romantic love, which eludes many. But no one can avoid death. It has been said that all the wars and plagues have never raised the death toll—it has always been one for each and every person. Yet we seem far less prepared for it than our ancestors. Why is that?

The Blessing of Modern Medicine

One reason is, paradoxically, that the great blessing of modern medicine has hidden death from us. Annie Dillard, in her novel *The Living*, devotes an entire page to the astonishing variety of ways death snatched the living from the midst of their homes and families without a moment's notice in the nineteenth century.

> Women took fever and died from hav-
> ing babies, and babies died from puni-
> ness or the harshness of the air. Men
> died from . . . rivers and horses, bulls,
> steam saws, mill gears, quarried rock, or
> falling trees or rolling logs. . . . Chil-
> dren lost their lives as . . . hard things
> smashed them, like trees and the
> ground when horses threw them, or
> they fell; they drowned in water; they
> sickened, and earaches wormed into
> their brains or fever from measles
> burned them up or pneumonia eased
> them out overnight.[3]

Death was something that people used to see

up close. To take just one example, the prominent British minister and theologian John Owen (1616–1683) outlived every one of his eleven children, as well as his first wife. Since people died where they lived, at home, Owen literally saw nearly every person he loved die before his eyes. The average family in the United States in colonial times lost one out of every three children before adulthood. And since the life expectancy of all people at that time was about forty years, great numbers lost their parents when they were still children. Nearly everyone grew up seeing corpses and watching relatives die, young and old.[4]

Medicine and science have relieved us of many causes of early death, and today the vast majority of people decline and die in hospitals and hospices, away from the eyes of others. It is normal now to live to adulthood and not watch anyone die, or even see a corpse except in the brief glance of an open coffin at a funeral.

Atul Gawande and others have pointed out that this hiddenness of dying in modern society means that we of all cultures live in denial of the inexorability of our impending death. Psalm 90:12 called readers to "number our days" that we may "gain a heart for wisdom." There has always been a danger that humans would live in denial of their own death. Of course we know intellectually and rationally that we are going to die, but deep down we repress it, we act as if we are going to live forever. And, according to the psalmist, that's *not wise.* It is the one absolute inevitability, yet modern people don't plan for it and don't live as if it is going to happen. We avoid doctors out of fear, denying the mortality of our bodies and assuming they will just go on forever. And yet in the face of imminent death we then demand unrealistic and extreme medical procedures.[5] We even find the discussion of death "in bad taste" or worse. Anthropologist Geoffrey Gorer, in his essay "The Pornography of Death," argued that in contemporary culture death has replaced sex as the new unmentionable.[6]

If people three thousand years ago had a problem with the denial of death, as Psalm 90 attests, then we have an infinitely greater one. Medical progress supports the illusion that death can be put off indefinitely. It is more rare than ever to find people who are, as the ancients were, reconciled to their own mortality. And there are even thinkers now who seriously believe death can be solved like any technological "performance issue."[7] Many in Silicon Valley are obsessed with overcoming mortality and living forever. All this means that modern people are more unrealistic and unprepared for death than any people in history.

This-world Happiness

A second reason that we today struggle so much with death is the secular age's requirement of this-world meaning and fulfillment. Anthropologist Richard Shweder surveys the ways non-Western and older cultures have helped their members face suffering.[8] They all did so by teaching their members about the meaning of life, the main thing for which every person should be living. Many societies believe that the main thing to live for is your people and family—children and grandchildren—in whom you live on after you die. Buddhism and many other ancient Eastern cultures have taught that the meaning of life is to see the illusory nature of this world and therefore to transcend it through an inner calmness and detachment of soul. Other cultures believe in reincarnation, or heaven or nirvana after death, and so one's main purpose is to live and believe in such a way that your soul journeys to heaven.

These all are quite different, and yet, Shweder argues, they had one thing in common. In each case the main thing to live for was something outside this material world and life, some object that suffering and death could not touch. It might be to go to heaven when you die, or to escape the cycle of reincarnation and go into eternal bliss, or to shed the illusion of the world and return to the All Soul of the universe, or to live an honorable life and be received at death into the company of your ancestors. But in each case, not only are tragedy and death unable to destroy your meaning in life, they can actually hasten the journey toward it, whether it is through spiritual growth, or the achievement of honor and virtue, or going into an eternity of joy.

Modern culture, however, is basically secular. Many today say that, because there is no God, soul, or spirit, no transcendent or supernatural dimension to reality, this material world is all there is. In that case, whatever gives your life meaning and purpose will have to be something within the confines of this earthly time frame. You must, as it were, rest your heart in something within the limited horizons of time and space. Whatever you decide will give meaning to your life will have to be some form of this-world happiness, comfort, or achievement. Or, at best, it might be a love relationship.

But death, of course, destroys all of these things. So while other cultures and worldviews see suffering and death as crucial chapters (and not the last) in your coherent life story, the secular view is completely different. Suffering is an interruption and death is the utter end. Shweder writes that for modern people, therefore:

> Suffering is . . . separated from the narrative structure of human life . . . a kind of "noise," an accidental interference into the life drama of the sufferer . . . Suffering [has] no intelligible relation to any plot, except as a chaotic interruption.[9]

Modern culture, then, is the worst in history at preparing its members for the only inevitability—death. When this limited meaning horizon comes together with the advance of medicine, it leaves many people paralyzed with anxiety and fear when confronted with a dying person.

Mark Ashton was vicar of St. Andrew the Great in Cambridge, England. At the age of sixty-two, in late 2008, he was diagnosed with inoperable gallbladder cancer. Because of his faith and joy in Christ, he showed a great deal of confidence in the face of dying and even a sense of anticipation, despite his keen recognition of the sadness of his family. During the next fifteen months, he talked with virtually everyone he met about his coming death with ease, eloquence, and poise. But this unnerved many people, who found not only his attitude but even his presence difficult to take.

He wrote: "Our age is so devoid of hope in the face of death that the topic has become unmentionable." He made a trip to a hairdresser in Eastbourne, where he engaged in conversation as usual with the woman who was cutting his hair. When she "asked me how I was and I replied that I had been told I had got just a few more months to live," the ordinary friendliness and chattiness of the place ceased. No matter how much he tried to talk to her, "I could not get another word out of her for the rest of the haircut."[10] Rather than accept and prepare for the inevitable, we only avert and deny it.

The Sense of Insignificance

A third reason modern secular culture has so much trouble with death is that, in redefining death as nonexistence, it has created a profound sense of insignificance. Ernest Becker, in the Pulitzer Prize–winning *The Denial of Death*, argues human beings cannot accept that all we are—our conscious self, our loves, our profound aspirations for beauty, goodness, truth—is going to cease to exist forever, in a literal blink of an eye. If death is truly the end—if we all die and eventually even the whole human civilization "dies" in the death of the sun—then nothing we do will make any final difference. If we come from nothing and go to nothing, how can we avoid, even now, a sense of nothingness? So he writes:

> The idea of death, the fear of it, haunts the human animal like nothing else; it is the mainspring of human activity—activity designed largely to avoid the

fatality of death, to overcome it by denying . . . that it is the final destiny.[11]

That fear of insignificance in the face of nonexistence *must* be dealt with in some way. Becker cites anthropologists who tell us ancient peoples were much less afraid of death, that death was "accompanied by rejoicing and festivities." He rightly adds that, while fear of death is a human universal, ancient people addressed it through belief in life and meaning after death. They believed in eternity, so that death was "the ultimate promotion." The problem for us today, however, is that "most modern Westerners have trouble believing this any more, which is what makes the fear of death so prominent a part of our psychological make-up."[12]

The rest of Becker's book is based on this

thesis; namely, that modern, secular culture has a problem with death that no other society has faced. He makes a case that the outsize place of so many things in modern culture—of sex and romance, of money and career, of politics and social causes—illustrates the ways that contemporary people seek to get a feeling of significance in the face of death without having recourse to God and religion.

Late-twentieth-century secular thinkers were, like Becker, quite aware that, as religion and faith in God receded, death would pose a problem. The existentialists, such as Albert Camus in "The Myth of Sisyphus," argued that the finality of death made life absurd and to try to deny this fact by losing yourself in pleasure and achievement was wrong.[13] An illustration may help here. Imagine someone has broken into your house, tied you up, and announced that he is going to kill you. For the sake of the illustration imagine also that you have absolutely no hope for rescue. What if he said, "I'm not heartless—tell me something you do that gives you a lot of happiness." You answer that you enjoy playing chess. "Well, let's play a game of chess before I kill you. Won't that make your final moments pleasant?" The only truthful answer would be that your impending death would drain all the satisfaction out of a game. Death takes away the significance and joy of things.

Becker goes further and says that this fear of death is something that is unique to us humans.

> It is a terrifying dilemma to be in and to
> have to live with. The lower animals are,
> of course, spared this painful contradic-
> tion, as they lack a symbolic identity and

the self-consciousness that goes with it. . . . The knowledge of death is reflective and conceptual, and animals are spared it. They [experience death as] a few minutes of fear, a few seconds of anguish, and it is over. But to live a whole lifetime with the fate of death haunting one's dreams and even the most sun-filled days—that's something else.[14]

More recent secular thinkers have not struck such dire notes. Drawing on the ancient philosophers Epicurus and Lucretius, many today argue that death is "nothing to be frightened of," and there is a constant stream of articles posted with that message, such as Jessica Brown's essay in *The Guardian* "We Fear Death, but What If Dying Isn't as Bad as We Think?"[15] After all, the reasoning goes, when you die you simply don't know anything or feel anything. There is no pain or anguish. Why be afraid of it? But efforts to say that modern people should find death no big deal have not worked for most. Philosopher Luc Ferry says it is "brutal" and dishonest to tell people facing death, and therefore the loss of all love relationships, that they should not fear it.[16] Dylan Thomas strikes a far more resonant chord with us when he says we should "Rage, rage against the dying of the light."[17]

Becker is right. The human race as a whole can't *not* fear and hate death. It is a unique and profound problem. Religion gave people tools to help in facing our most formidable foe, and modern secularism has not come up with anything to compensate for its loss.

A Fear of Judgment

A fourth reason why we struggle today with death is the loss of categories for sin, guilt, and forgiveness in modern culture. Friedrich Nietzsche argued that the idea and feeling of "indebtedness" or guilt emerged in human beings along with a belief in a transcendent God or gods to whom we must give obedience. But now, he said happily, as religion recedes and increasing numbers do not believe in a God of judgment, there would be a decline in our sense of guilt. Atheism could even mean "a second innocence."[18]

Wilfred M. McClay, in "The Strange Persistence of Guilt," argues that Nietzsche's prediction has not come true.[19] Freud, McClay says, was a better prophet when he said that guilt is an irreplaceable feature of any civilization. It is the price we must pay if we are going to restrain the kind of selfish behavior that undermines societies. That means that even if we try to end our sense of sinfulness and guilt, it will persist and take other forms. "Guilt is crafty, a trickster and chameleon, capable of disguising itself, hiding out, changing its size and appearance . . . all the while managing to persist and deepen."[20] Freud called guilt *unbehagen*. The word means "malaise," a strong sense of uneasiness about oneself and life itself, which leads to a drumbeat of questions: "Why isn't life better? Why don't I fit in? Why do I feel the need to work so hard to prove myself? Will anybody really love me?"

Our secular culture believes Nietzsche rather than Freud at this point and has done all it can to liberate individuals in order to indulge in complete freedom of self-expression. That means removing the words "sin" and "guilt" from public discourse so everyone can be free to create and perform the self they choose. But this has left us in a strange position. As one scholar put it, we see evil and sin around us, things "that our culture no longer gives us the vocabulary to express," and so "a gulf has opened up in our culture between the visibility of evil and the intellectual resources available for coping with it."[21]

Many have pointed out that today our society is as moralistic and judgmental as it ever has been. We live in a "call-out culture" in which people are categorized reductionistically to good or evil and then are publicly shamed until they lose jobs and communities.[22] People are charged for what used to be called sins and are punished and banished in ways that look remarkably like religious ceremonial purification rites.

As McClay points out, human beings cannot

abandon their moral reflexes—a belief in moral absolutes, in sin and judgment, and in the imposition of guilt and shame. However, today we have abandoned the old underlying beliefs in God, heaven, and hell, and therefore have lost the older resources for repentance, showing grace, and granting forgiveness.[23]

All this triggers a crisis for modern people in the face of death. As a pastor I've spent many hours in the presence of dying people. As death approaches, people look back on their life and feel tremendous regret. The *unbehagen*, or deep dissatisfaction with oneself, comes to the fore. There may be guilt for things not said or done for loved ones, for apologies not made or received, for kindnesses refused or unkindnesses done and now beyond forgiveness, for wasted opportunities or even a wasted life.

But beyond regret for the past, there is also

fear of the future. T. S. Eliot writes: "Not what we call death, but what beyond death is not death / We fear, we fear."[24] Behind and beneath all the other emotions is the fear of judgment. In 1 Corinthians 15, Saint Paul's lengthy discussion of death, he asserts that the "sting of death" is sin (verse 56). Just as he had taught in Romans 1:20–22, we all know in our hearts, however deeply hidden, that God is our Creator and the one who deserves our worship and obedience. But we have "suppressed" (verse 18) that knowledge in order to claim sovereignty over our own lives.

Death, however, makes our self-dissatisfaction much more conscious. Our conscience cannot be silenced as it was before. Shakespeare's Hamlet thinks about suicide, but he decides not to do it. He dreads something after death, "the undiscovered country from whose bourn no traveler returns," which leads us to fear judgment. So we "bear those ills we have, [rather] than fly to others that we know not of" because "conscience does make cowards of us all."[25]

Despite all the efforts, there is a persistence of guilt, and never more than when we face death. Modern culture gives us little to deal with this, but the Christian faith has some astonishing resources for us.

Our Champion

Rather than living in fear of death, we should see it as spiritual smelling salts that will awaken us out of our false belief that we will live forever. When you are at a funeral, especially one for a friend or a loved one, listen to God speaking to you, telling you that everything in life is temporary except for His love. This is reality.

Everything in this life is going to be taken away from us, except one thing: God's love, which can go into death with us and take us through it and into His arms. It's the one thing you can't lose. Without God's love to embrace us, we will always feel radically insecure, and we ought to be.

One of my theology professors, Addison Leitch, told the class about speaking at a missionary conference. Two young women hearing his preaching decided they wanted to give their lives to missionary service. Both sets of their parents were extremely upset with Dr. Leitch, who they felt had filled their children with religious fanaticism. They said to him, "You know that there is no security in being a missionary. The

pay is low, the living situation may be danger-
ous. We've tried talking to our daughters. They
need to get a job and a career, maybe get a master's degree or something like that so that they
have some security before they go off and do
this missionary thing."

And this is what Dr. Leitch told them: "You
want them to have some security? We're all on a
little ball of rock called Earth, and we're spin-
ning through space at millions of miles an hour.
Someday a trapdoor is going to open up under
every single one of us, and we will fall through
it. And either there will be millions and millions of miles of nothing—or else there will be
the everlasting arms of God. And you want
them to get a master's degree to give them a little security?"[26]

It's in death that God says, "If I'm not your
security, then you've got no security, because

I'm the only thing that can't be taken away from you. I will hold you in my everlasting arms. Every other set of arms will fail you, but I will never fail you."

Smelling salts are very disagreeable, but they are also effective. But as you're waking from your illusions, be at peace, because here's what Jesus Christ offers to us if by faith we have him as our Savior.

In the book of Hebrews we read:

> In bringing many sons and daughters to glory, it was fitting that God, for whom and through whom everything exists, should make the pioneer of their salvation perfect through what he suffered. . . . He too shared in their humanity so that by his death he might

break the power of him who holds the power of death—that is, the devil—and free those who all their lives were held in slavery by their fear of death. (Hebrews 2:10, 14–15)

In order to save us, Jesus became the "pioneer" of our salvation through suffering and death. The Greek word here is *archēgos*. Bible scholar William Lane says it really ought to be translated "our champion."[27]

A champion was somebody who engaged in representative combat. When David fought Goliath, they both fought as champions for their respective armies. They fought as substitutes. If your champion won, the whole army won the battle, even though none of them lifted a finger. That is what Jesus did. He took on our greatest enemies—sin and death. Unlike David, he didn't just risk his life, he gave his life, but in doing so he defeated them. He took the penalty we deserve for our sins—the punishment of death—in our place, as our substitute. But because he himself was a man of perfect, sinless love for God and neighbor, death could not hold him (Acts 2:24). He rose from the dead.

That's why in Hebrews 2:14, the writer says he destroyed the power of death because he died for us, taking away our penalty and guaranteeing the future resurrection of all who unite with him by faith. Jesus Christ, our great captain and champion, has killed death.

All religions talk about death and the afterlife, but in general they proclaim that you must lead a good life in order to be ready for eternity. Yet as death approaches we all know we have not even come close to doing our best; we have not lived as we ought. So we stay, with warrant, enslaved by the fear of death until the end.

Christianity is different. It doesn't leave you to face death on your own, by holding up your life record and hoping it will suffice. Instead it gives you a champion who has defeated death, who pardons you and covers you with his love. You face death "in him" and with *his* perfect record (Philippians 3:9). To the degree we believe, know, and embrace that, we are released from the power of death.

So when Hamlet spoke of death as "the undiscovered country from whose bourn no traveler returns" he was wrong. Someone *has* come back from death. Jesus Christ has destroyed the power of death and "a cleft has opened in the pitiless walls of the world" for us.[28] When by faith we grasp this, we need fear darkness no more.

Saint Paul wrote the famous lines:

> Where, O death, is your victory?
> Where, O death, is your sting?
> (1 Corinthians 15:55)

Paul is not facing death stoically. He's *taunting* it. How can anyone in his right mind look at humanity's most powerful enemy *and taunt it*? Paul immediately gives the answer: "The sting of death is sin, and the power of sin is the law. But thanks be to God! He gives us the victory through our Lord Jesus Christ" (1 Corinthians 15:56–57). Paul says that the "sting of death" (as Hamlet says) is our conscience, our sense of sin and judgment before the moral law. But Christ has taken it away—or more accurately, taken it upon himself for all who believe.

Donald Grey Barnhouse was the minister of

Tenth Presbyterian Church in Philadelphia when his wife, only in her late thirties, died of cancer, leaving him with four children under the age of twelve. When driving with his children to the funeral, a large truck pulled past them in the left lane, casting its shadow over them. Barnhouse asked all in the car, "Would you rather be run over by the truck or the shadow of the truck?" His eleven-year-old answered, "Shadow, of course." Their father concluded, "Well, that's what has happened to your mother. . . . Only the shadow of death has passed over her, because death itself ran over Jesus."[29]

The sting of death is sin, and the poison went into Jesus.

So any Christian man or woman has the power to triumph over death like this. Once I was speaking to a friend about his chronically ill wife, who over and over again had defied medical predictions and had "beaten death." Now she was very ill again, with a real possibility that this time she would not pull through. Talking with her husband, we agreed that no matter what happened a believer *always* beats death whether they die or not. Jesus Christ has defeated death, and now all it can do is make us more happy and loved than we've ever been. If Jesus died for you and he has risen to be your living Savior, then what can death do to you?

The Rupture
of Death

Do Not Grieve Like
Those Without Hope

Brothers and sisters, we do not want you to . . .
grieve like the rest of mankind, who have no hope.
For we believe that Jesus died and rose again, and
so we believe that God will bring with Jesus those
who have fallen asleep in him.

—1 THESSALONIANS 4:13–14

I n our first chapter we talked about how to
face your own death without fear. But how
do we face the death of loved ones? I can say
without fear of contradiction there will be a lot

of death in your future. If you are fortunate enough to live a long life, you will be encountering death more and more as you go on—the death of not just associates but friends, and not just friends but dearly loved ones. In 1 Thessalonians 4 we are told that Christianity gives us remarkable resources—not only for your own death, but for the loss of people we love.

In the epigraph above, Saint Paul tells his friends: "I don't want you to grieve like the rest of humanity, who have no hope." That's a double negative. He is actually saying, "I want you to *grieve hopefully*." Saint Paul is calling for an extreme balance before our Great Enemy. When we think of someone who is "balanced" that usually means a person who avoids extremes, but Paul is calling us to a balanced combination *of* two extremes. Notice he does not say, "Don't grieve." He wants Christians to grieve when loved ones die, but in a particular way. He says neither, "Instead of grieving I want you to have hope," nor "There's really no hope, so just cry and grieve." Rather, he says Christians can and must both grieve profoundly and fully and yet do so with hope. How does that work?

We Are to Grieve

On the one hand we are to grieve rather than take the stoic approach. But although grieving is right, grief can become bitterness; it can embitter you, darken your life, and stifle joy unless you season it with hope. The most remarkable example of this is Jesus at the tomb of Lazarus, his friend, in John 11. Jesus did not come up to Mary and Martha, the bereaved sisters, and say, "There, there. Keep a stiff upper lip. Chin up.

Be strong." He didn't do any of that. When Mary speaks to him, we are told, in the shortest verse in the Bible, "Jesus wept" (John 11:35). He doesn't speak—all he does is weep. And then, when he goes to Lazarus's tomb (though all the English translations mute this), we are told that Jesus was "snorting with rage" (John 11:38).[1]

Here is Jesus, the Son of God, who knew quite well that he was going to do a great miracle and raise his friend from the dead. We would think, would we not, that he would be walking to the tomb quietly smiling and thinking to himself, "Wait till you see what I'm going to do! Everything is going to be fine!" Instead he is weeping, grieving, angry.

How could the Creator of the world be angry at something in his world? Only if death is an intruder. Death was not in God's original design for the world and human life. Look at the first three chapters of Genesis. We were not meant to die; we were meant to last. We were meant to get more and more beautiful as time goes on, not more and more enfeebled. We were meant to get stronger, not to weaken and die. Paul explains elsewhere, in Romans 8:18–23, that when we turned from God to be our own Lords and Saviors, everything broke. Our bodies, the natural order, our hearts, our relationships—nothing works the way it was originally designed. It is all marred, distorted, broken, and death is part of that (Genesis 3:7–19). So Jesus weeps and is angry at the monstrosity of death. It is a deep distortion of the creation he loves.

Therefore, the stoic, "keep a stiff upper lip" reaction to death and grief is wrong. There are many versions of this. One goes like this: "Now, now. He is with the Lord. The Lord works all things together for good. There's no need to weep too much. Of course you will miss him, but he's in heaven now. And everything happens for a reason." Technically there may be nothing wrong with any of these statements. They may be true. But Jesus knew all of them as well. He knew Lazarus was going to be raised. He knew that this was part of the Father's plan for his ministry. And he was still grieving with sorrow and anger. Why? Because that is the right response to the evil and unnaturalness of death.

Most secular advice for the bereaved is some version of stoicism. An ancient example is in the *Iliad*, where Achilles tells the father of the fallen Hector, "Bear up . . . Nothing will come of sorrowing for your son."[2] Modern skeptics will say, "Look, death is the end, and that's it. Grieving about it makes no difference. It doesn't help a thing. It is what it is."

A somewhat more sophisticated modern version of the secular view tells us to look at death as a perfectly natural part of the life cycle. It says: "Death is natural. Death is just a part of life. Death is nothing to be afraid of. Our bodies enrich the earth like the grass, trees, and other animals when we die. Eventually we become stardust. We're still part of the universe. It's okay." But does such a view of death fit our deepest intuitions?

Peter Kreeft is a Christian philosopher who tells a story about a couple who were friends of his and who were not religious people. They had a seven-year-old son whose three-year-old cousin had died.

So they sat down and tried to comfort him. They said, "You realize death is perfectly natural." They were trying to help him by explaining, "Death is fine, it is perfectly natural. When you die, your body goes to the earth and enriches the earth and other things grow. Remember, you watched *The Lion King*."

But instead of being comforted, the little boy ran out of the room screaming, "I don't want him to be fertilizer!"[3]

The little boy was closer to Jesus's point of view than his parents were. He was grieving. Death is not right. It's not the way it ought to be. It's not the way God made the world.

To say, "Oh, death is just natural," is to harden and perhaps kill a part of your heart's hope that makes you human. We know deep down that we are not like trees or grass. We were created to *last*. We don't want to be ephemeral, to be inconsequential. We don't want to just be a wave upon the sand. The deepest desires of our hearts are for love that lasts.

Death is not the way it ought to be. It is abnormal, it is not a friend, it isn't right. This isn't truly part of the circle of life. Death is the end of it. So grieve. Cry. The Bible tells us not only to weep, but to weep with those who are weeping (Romans 12:15 NASB). We have a lot of crying to do.

We Are to Grieve with Hope

However, though we are definitely right to grieve, Saint Paul says we must grieve with hope. As we have seen, to suppress grief and outrage at death is not only bad for us psychologically, it's actually bad for our humanity. Yet anger can dehumanize us, too, making us bitter and hard. Which means that we cannot *only* "rage against the dying of the light." We also need a hope that influences how we grieve.

But what is there to hope for? Look at Jesus Christ at the tomb of his friend Lazarus. He's grieving, he's weeping, and he's angry, even though he knows that in a few minutes he will raise his friend from the dead.

But he knows something that no one else could even imagine. At the end of chapter 11 of John, after he raised his friend Lazarus from the dead, all of his opponents said, "Well, that's the last straw. We've got to kill him now. We've got to kill Jesus."

Jesus knew that to raise Lazarus from the dead would push his enemies toward extreme measures. So he knew that the only way he could get Lazarus out of the tomb was if he put himself into it. Indeed, if he is to guarantee resurrection for all who believe in him, he must put himself into the grave. On the Cross that's what he did.

Because of Jesus's death, we are released from sin and death, and share in his resurrection, as it says in Romans 6:5–9:

> For if we have been united with him in a death like his, we will certainly also be united with him in a resurrection like his. For we know that our old self was crucified with him so that the body ruled by sin might be done away with, that we should no longer be slaves to sin—because anyone who has died has been set free from sin. Now if we died with Christ, we believe that we will also live with him. For we know that since Christ was raised from the dead, he cannot die again; death no longer has mastery over him.

Jesus conquered death, and we will share in his resurrection. That's our hope.

If you don't have that hope, I'm not sure what you do when you are in the presence of death. You can let it fester and cause despair. Or we can add hope to our grief.

We tend to see grief and hope as mutually exclusive, but Paul does not. An illustration may help to see how these can go together. For many years, people preserved meat by salting it. (If you have ever had country ham you know this is still a method of preservation.) Salt cured the meat so it didn't decay.

Similarly, unless you salt your grief with hope, your grief will go bad.

When we grieve and rage in the face of death, we are responding appropriately to a great evil. But Christians have a hope that can be "rubbed into" our sorrow and anger the way salt is rubbed into meat. Neither stifling grief nor giving way to despair is right. Neither repressed anger nor unchecked rage is good for your soul. But pressing hope into your grief makes you wise, compassionate, humble, and tenderhearted.

Grieve fully yet with profound hope! Do you see why I said that this is not some midpoint moderation but a combination of extremes? This will give you more strength than stoicism and more freedom to lament than hopelessness.

I had my first personal experience of this many years ago. There was a nodule on my thyroid gland that was being biopsied. I was in the clinic when the pathologist said to me, "You have a carcinoma." The shocked look on my face was the reason she then said, "I'm sure it's treatable!" My thyroid cancer turned out to indeed be treatable. Nevertheless, over the next

few months I learned that it is one thing to tell
people "Christians have hope in the face of
death," and it's another thing to grasp that hope
personally and practically when you know you
have a cancer that can kill you.

I discovered that one of the keys to getting ac-
cess to this Christian hope was to ponder what
Saint Paul said about how he didn't want his
friends to grieve "like the rest of mankind, who
have no hope." Some commentators have pointed
out that there are many religions and almost all
of them believe in some kind of life after death.
So how can Paul say that the rest of the human
race has no hope in the face of death?

As others have pointed out, Paul is speaking
relatively. When Jesus says in Luke 14:26 that
his followers should "hate father and mother"
he means their devotion to him should be so

great that it makes all other loyalties pale and look like hate in comparison. Likewise Paul is not saying that no one has any expectation of life after death, but that the Christian future hope is uniquely powerful. He is calling us to delight in the greatness of our hope in order to prepare ourselves for death.

The Power of Christian Hope

What then are some of the features of this unique hope we have in the face of death?

Personal Hope

It's a personal hope. The future of those who die in Christ is a world of infinite love. There are religions that say, "Yes, there is life after death, but you lose your personal consciousness. You lose your sense of individuality, which was an illusion anyway. It's like you're a drop going back into the ocean. You don't remain a drop. You just become part of the All Soul. There is not a *you* or a *me* after death, but you continue as part of the universe."

But Paul goes on to say:

> For the Lord himself will come down from heaven, with a loud command, with the voice of the archangel and with the trumpet call of God, and the dead in Christ will rise first. After that, we who are still alive and are left will be caught up together with them in the clouds to meet the Lord in the air. And so we will be with the Lord forever.

Therefore encourage each other with these words. (Thessalonians 4:16–18)

Notice all the references that we will be *with* one another. You will be with people you've lost. And do you see the word "together"? We will be with the Lord together forever. These are words that mean personal relationships—perfect relationships of love that go on forever.

Jonathan Edward's famous sermon "Heaven Is a World of Love" begins by arguing that the greatest happiness we can know is to be loved by another person, and yet, he adds, on earth the greatest love relationships are like a pipe so clogged that only a little water (or love) actually gets through. In heaven, however, all these "clogs" are removed and the love we will experience will be infinitely, inexpressibly greater than anything we have known here.[4] On earth we hide behind facades for fear of being rejected, but that means we never experience the transforming power of being fully known yet truly loved at the same time. In addition, we love selfishly and enviously, which disrupts, weakens, and even ends love relationships. Finally, our love relationships are darkened by the fear of losing the other person, which can make us so controlling that we often drive people away, or in other cases become fearful of making any commitments at all.

Edwards concludes by declaring that all of these things that reduce love in this world to a trickle at the bottom of a riverbed are removed when we get to heaven, where love is an endless deluge and fountain of delight and bliss flowing in and out of us infinitely and eternally.

The Christian hope is for a personal future of love relationships.

Material Hope

Our hope is also material. Notice that Paul does not say merely that we will go to heaven. He says that the "dead in Christ will rise." Yes, we believe our souls go to heaven when we die, but that isn't the climactic end of our salvation. At the end of all things, we will get new bodies. We will be raised like Jesus was raised. Remember that when the risen Jesus met his disciples he insisted that he had "flesh and bones," that he was not a spirit. He ate in front of them to prove the point (Luke 24:37–43). He taught them that, unlike all other major religions, Christianity promises not a spirit-only future, but a renewed heavens and earth, a perfected material world from which all suffering and tears, disease, evil, injustice, and death have been eliminated.

Our future is not an immaterial one. We are not going to float in the kingdom of God like ghosts. We're going to walk, eat, hug, and be hugged. We're going to love. We're going to sing, because we're going to have vocal cords. And we will do all this in degrees of joy, excellence, satisfaction, beauty, and power we cannot now imagine. We're going to eat and drink with the Son of Man.

And this is the final defeat of death. This is not merely a consolation in heaven for the material life we lost. This is a restoration of that life. It's getting the love, the body, the mind, the being we've always longed for.

You see, there's a real you, a true self down inside you, but then there are all the flaws and weaknesses that bury and mar and hide it. But the Christian hope is that the love and holiness of God will burn it all away. On that day, we're going to see each other, and say, "I always knew you could be like this. I saw glimpses of it. I saw flashes of it. Now look at you."

Paul, knowing something about the other cultures and religions of the world, says our future is not an impersonal, immaterial world of abstract spirituality, but a personal future of love relationships and the restoration of all things.

If the knowledge of this future was always present in our minds, would we become as downcast as we do? Why ever think of payback for people who have wronged you when you know you're going to get not just all you've ever wanted, but more than you dare ask or think? Why envy anyone? This hope is transforming.

Beatific Hope

Along with personal hope and material hope, there is beatific hope. Paul does not say we will simply be together with others. Nor does he talk so much about how lovely the world will be when it's healed. That's not the main thing in his mind. Here's the final note, the biggest emphasis—that we will be "with *the Lord* forever" (1 Thessalonians 4:17). It means we will be in perfect communion with him, we will see the Lord face-to-face. This is what has been historically called the "beatific vision."

Paul talks about it in 1 Corinthians 13:12 when he says, "For now we see only a reflection as in a mirror; then we shall see face to face. Now I know in part; then I shall know fully, even as I am fully known." John speaks of it in 1 John 3:2 when he says, "We know that when

Christ appears, we shall be like him, for we shall see him as he is." When we look into the face of Christ it will completely transform us because, as Paul says, we will finally be fully known yet fully loved.

When Moses asked in fear and trembling to see God's glory (Exodus 33:18), God replied that for any human being to see God's glory directly would be fatal (Exodus 33:19–20). Sinful human beings cannot come into the presence of a holy God and live. But Moses certainly knew the danger. Why did he seek this direct sight of God's glory anyway? Because he intuitively knew that we were originally created to know and love God supremely, to commune with his love and see his beauty. Moses knew at some level that our human restlessness and drive— for approval, comfort, aesthetic experience, love, power, accomplishment—are all ways of filling what Saint Augustine famously called the "God-shaped hole" in us. In every set of arms we are seeking God's arms, in every loving face we are seeking God's face, in every accomplishment we are looking for God's approval.

Moses was after the beatific vision, the direct, face-to-face relationship with God we were made for. God's answer to Moses is essentially the theme of the rest of the Bible and of the gospel itself. God told him that he would have to be covered or hidden in the cleft of a rock so he would only be able to see God's "back" (Exodus 33:19–23). In the Old Testament we see God's glory residing in the tabernacle's Holy of Holies, present among his people but largely inaccessible.

But when Jesus comes, John announces that in Christ "we beheld his glory" (John 1:14), and Paul adds that because of Jesus's death and work on our behalf, those of us who believe in him get a foretaste, by faith, of that future trans-forming vision. He writes:

> For God, who said, "Let light shine out of darkness," made his light shine in our hearts to give us the light of the knowledge of God's glory displayed in the face of Christ. (2 Corinthians 4:6)

This is not the direct, face-to-face encounter that Moses asked for and that Paul and John say is still in the future. Rather it is a "faith-sight" that we can have now. We cannot see God's glory yet with our physical eyes, but through faith, the Word and the Spirit can give us a powerful sense of his presence and reality in our lives and hearts. Sometimes we read the promises and truths of Scripture and Jesus becomes overpoweringly real and consoling to us. Paul talks of it like this:

> And we all, who with unveiled faces contemplate the Lord's glory, are being transformed into his image with ever-increasing glory, which comes from the Lord, who is the Spirit. (2 Corinthians 3:18)

What Paul is talking about is far more rare than it should be, but it is not an experience reserved for a few saints. In Romans he writes: "Hope does not put us to shame, because God's love has been poured out into our hearts through the Holy Spirit, who has been given to us" (Romans 5:5). Our future hope, he argues, is strengthened the more we do not merely know intellectually about the love of God but

have it poured into our heart—experienced—
through the Holy Spirit. Many have felt what
Paul is talking about. You may be reading the
Bible or praying or singing his praise and you
get a sense of his greatness and love. It is only
partial, only by faith, but it comforts and
changes you. It's the light of his face shining in
our hearts. William Cowper wrote:

> Sometimes a light surprises
> The Christian while he sings;
> It is the Lord Who rises
> With healing in His wings.[5]

C. S. Lewis says if these lower reaches of the
stream of God's glory are so intoxicating, what
will it be like to drink from the fountainhead?[6]

This is what we are built for. Psalm 16 ends
with a sentence that says, literally, "In your face is
fullness of joy. At your right hand are pleasures

forevermore" (Psalm 16:11). Psalm 17:15 says that after death, "When I awake I will be satisfied with seeing your likeness." John Flavel, a British minister and theologian from the seventeenth century, wrote about Psalm 17:15 and the vision of God that is in our future. He said:

> It will be a satisfying sight (Psalm 17:15). . . . The understanding can know no more, the will can will no more, the affections of joy, delight, and love are at full rest and quiet in their proper center. . . . All that delights you in earthly things can never satisfy you—for all your desires are eminently for God himself. . . . The comforts you had here are but only drops inflaming, not satisfying, the appetites of your soul: but *the Lamb . . . shall lead them to*

fountains of living waters. (Revelation 7:17)[7]

Kathy sometimes says to me, "One of the great things about future glory is you don't have to buy souvenirs." Do you know what she means? You don't live with regrets. You don't say, "I never got any photos when I went to that country," or "I never had this or that experience." Anything wonderful or great in this world is only an echo or foretaste of what is present in the Vision of God and in the New Heaven and New Earth, the world of love.

When at last you see the God of the universe looking at you with love, all of the potentialities of your soul will be released and you will experience the glorious freedom of the children of God.

Assured Hope

There is one more aspect of hope available to Christians that is unique. While other religions may have a belief in an afterlife, there is no firm assurance offered as to who will enjoy it. Theocritus wrote: "Hopes are for the living; the dead are without hope."[8] Other religions can offer no person an assurance that they are virtuous enough to merit a good existence in the next life.[9]

However, Paul writes:

> We believe that Jesus died and rose again, and so we believe that God will bring with Jesus those who have fallen asleep in him. (1 Thessalonians 4:14)

What is Paul talking about? The wages of sin

is death (Romans 6:23)—that is what we deserve. When a prisoner has fully paid his debt he is released; the law no longer has any claim on him. So when Jesus fully paid the debt of sin with his death, he was resurrected. The law and death had no more claim on him. Nor does it have any claim on us if we believe in him. "There is now no condemnation for those who are in Christ Jesus" (Romans 8:1). When we put our faith in him we are as free from condemnation as if we had paid the penalty ourselves—as if we had died. "Now if we died with Christ, we believe that we shall also live with him" (Romans 6:8). That's what Paul is saying here in 1 Thessalonians 4. We not only know about the future world of love, the vision of God, and a renewed universe. We are assured that these astounding things are ours. We do not anxiously wonder if we have been good enough to be with

God when we die. We live with deep assurance of all of these things. This, too, is part of our unequaled Christian hope.

What more could we ask for?

In Mark, chapter 5, Jesus is brought into a room with a little dead girl. Everybody else is wailing in grief, but he's calm. He sits down and he takes her by the hand. The eyewitness account preserves the actual Aramaic words that Jesus Christ spoke to her. He said, *Talitha koum*, which is best translated, "Honey, get up." And she got up.

Jesus sits down, takes her by the hand, and speaks to her the way any father or mother would speak to a child on a sunny morning. Jesus says, "Honey, it's time to get up."

What is Jesus Christ facing at that moment? He is facing the most formidable, inexorable, implacable force that the human race has to face: death.

And with a little tug of his hand, he lifts her right up through it! It's his way of saying, "If I have you by the hand, if you know me through faith in grace, nothing can hurt you. Even death itself, when it comes to you, will just be like waking from a nice night's sleep. If I have you by the hand, even death, when it comes upon you, will only make you something greater. Nothing can hurt you. Be at peace."

C. S. Lewis says, "He will make the feeblest and filthiest of us into . . . a dazzling, radiant, immortal creature, pulsating all through with such energy and joy and wisdom and love as we cannot now imagine, a bright stainless mirror which reflects back to God perfectly (though, of course, on a smaller scale) His own boundless power and delight and goodness. . . . That is what we are in for. Nothing less."[10]

We Are to Laugh and Sing for Joy

In our culture one of the few places where it is acceptable to talk about death is at a funeral. People attend funerals for different reasons. One, of course, is to honor the person who has died and to pay tribute to a unique life. But also your mind is forced to dwell on ultimate things. Just as people think about their own weddings (either in remembrance or in anticipation) when attending a wedding, a funeral confronts you with the fact that one day it will be your funeral people are attending. This tends to turn minds toward questions of the reality of God and the afterlife, even if those thoughts usually don't arise. But after the funeral is over, unless the deceased was a close family member or friend, the mind goes back to its default setting to keep thoughts about death as far away as possible.

At a funeral service (as opposed to a memorial service) we are literally in the presence of death. There is a dead body in that coffin. While people have many reactions to being in the presence of death, there are two opposite mistakes we can make: One is to despair too much; the other is to shrug it off and not learn what we should from it.

Neither will be of much benefit to you, so we must do as the Bible tells us to do: We should grieve, yet we should have hope; we should wake up from our denial and discover a source of peace that will not leave us; and finally, we should laugh and sing.

The Bible says that when the Son of God

returns, the mountains and the woods will sing for joy. When the Son of God rises with healing in his wings, when Jesus Christ comes back, the Bible says the mountains and the trees will sing for joy, because in his hands we finally become everything God intended us to be.

And if it's true that the mountains and the trees will sing for joy, what will we be able to do?

One of the great expressions of the Christian hope in literature is a poem by George Herbert, a seventeenth-century Christian poet. He wrote a poem called "A Dialogue-Anthem." With elegance and power it imagines a dialogue between Death and a Christian, based on 1 Corinthians 15.

DIALOGUE-ANTHEM
by George Herbert

CHRISTIAN: *Alas, poor Death! Where is thy glory?*
Where is thy famous force, thy ancient sting?

DEATH: Alas, poor mortal, void of story!
Go spell and read how I have kill'd thy King.

CHRISTIAN: *Poor death! and who was hurt*
thereby?
Thy curse being laid on him makes thee ac-
curst.

DEATH: Let losers talk, yet thou shalt die:
These arms shall crush thee.

CHRISTIAN: *Spare not, do thy worst. I shall*
be one day better than before: Thou so
much worse, that thou shalt be no more.

Here's the Christian looking at Death and
saying, "Come on, spare not, do thy worst,

come on. Hit me with your best shot. The lower you lay me, the higher you will raise me. The harder you hit me, the more brilliant and glorious I'll be." Elsewhere George Herbert says, "Death used to be an executioner, but the Gospel makes him just a gardener." Death used to be able to crush us, but now all death can do is plant us in God's soil so we become something extraordinary.

Years ago, when the famous Chicago minister Dwight Moody was dying, he said: "Pretty soon you're going to read in the Chicago papers that Dwight Moody is dead. Don't you believe it. I will be more alive than I am right now."

Grieve with hope; wake up and be at peace; laugh in the face of death, and sing for joy at what's coming. If Jesus Christ has you by the hand, you can sing.

A Prayer

Our Father, you are the strength of your people, and we ask now that you would heal the brokenhearted among us and bind up their wounds. We ask that you would grant to them and to all else the vision of that life in which all tears are wiped away and all shadows have fled away.

Raise us up in your Spirit's power now to follow you in hope and trust, and give us your loving power to protect us, your wise power to nurture us, your beauty to enrapture us, your peace to fulfill us, and lift up our hearts in the light and love of your presence. And we ask in the name of the one who is the Resurrection and the Life, Jesus Christ. Amen.

Appendix

If you are facing
your own possible death

The Christian faith gives believers unparalleled promises and hopes in the face of death. We should always be in prayer for healing, because we have an all-powerful, prayer-hearing God. But we should also be ready to meet God face-to-face at any time. This is our opportunity to do both—prayer and preparation.

Do you believe that Jesus came to be your Savior, to live the life you should have lived and also to die in your place in order to atone for your sins and provide salvation as a free gift of grace? Have you turned and repented for all you have done wrong? Do you trust and rest in him alone for your acceptance before God?

If you have this faith, then you will not face God's condemnation (Romans 8:1).

If you're still having trouble experiencing God's comfort and assurance of love in the face of death, ask yourself: Are you clear in your mind about the difference between salvation by faith in Christ's work and record rather than your own? Could it be that in subtle ways your heart still clings in part to the belief that we need to earn our salvation? Then memories of past moral failures will darken your heart. Refuse those thoughts and meditate on Philippians 3:4–9. Paul says here that if anyone should have "confidence in the flesh"—the belief that good works could merit eternal life—it should be him. He was the most religiously and morally zealous person that he knew of. But he realized that all of these things were useless. All that matters is to "be found in him, not having a righteousness [moral record] of my own that comes from the law, but that which is through faith in Christ—the righteousness that comes from God on the basis of faith."

There are many biblical promises for believers to meditate on as they face death. Here are some texts to consider over the course of a week when contemplating or facing your own death. There are seven—one for each day:

Monday. "I eagerly expect and hope that I will in no way be ashamed, but will have sufficient courage so that now as always Christ will be exalted in my body, whether by life or by death. For to me, to live is Christ and to die is gain. If I am to go on living in the body, this will mean fruitful labor for me. Yet what shall I choose? I do not know! I am torn between the two" (Philippians 1:20–23). *While the Bible tells us that death is a tragic monstrosity, yet for Christians with assurance of their relationship with God, it is a win-win. There are unique ways to serve and enjoy God both here and in heaven. Paul is not lying when he says he is "torn between the two."*

Tuesday. "But now, this is what the LORD says— . . . 'Do not fear, for I have redeemed you; I have summoned you by name; you are mine. When you pass through the waters, I will be with you; and when you pass through the rivers, they will not sweep over you. When you walk through the fire, you will not be burned; the flames will not set you ablaze. For I am the

LORD your God, the Holy One of Israel, your Savior'" (Isaiah 43:1–3). *God is saying plainly that, if we are his, he will never let us go. When we suffer here, it will only make us into something more beautiful, the way that pressure creates a diamond. And if we die, it is merely a dark door into ultimate joy. Consider this hymn, based on Isaiah 43.*

> *That soul that on Jesus has leaned for repose*
> *I will not, I will not desert to its foes.*
> *That soul though all hell should endeavor to shake*
> *I'll never, no never, no never forsake.*[1]

Wednesday. "Therefore we do not lose heart. Though outwardly we are wasting away, yet inwardly we are being renewed day by day. For our light and momentary troubles are achieving for us an eternal glory that far outweighs them all. So we fix our eyes not on what is seen, but on what is unseen, since what is seen is temporary, but what is unseen is eternal" (2 Corinthians 4:16–18). *If we live to old age we can feel our bodies (and our beauty) fading, yet if we are growing in God's grace, our souls, as it were, are becoming stronger and more beautiful. At death this reversal becomes complete. Our bodies disintegrate and we become blindingly glorious. Comfort yourself with these words.*

Thursday. "For we know that if the earthly tent we live in is destroyed, we have a building from God, an eternal house in heaven, not built by human hands. . . . For while we are in this tent, we groan and are burdened, because we do not wish to be unclothed but to be clothed instead with our heavenly dwelling, so that what is mortal may be swallowed up by life. . . . We are confident, I say, and would prefer to be away from the body and at home with the LORD. So we make it our goal to please him, whether we are at home in the body or away from it" (2 Corinthians 5:1, 4, 8–9). *It is reported that an army chaplain, comforting a frightened soldier before a battle, told him: "If you live, Jesus will be with you, but if you die, you will be with him. Either way he has you."*

Friday. "Do not let your hearts be troubled. You believe in God; believe also in me. My Father's house has many rooms; if that were not so, would I have told you that I am going there to prepare a place for you? And if I go and prepare a place for you, I will come back and take you to be with me that you also may be where

I am. . . . Peace I leave with you; my peace I give you. I do not give to you as the world gives. Do not let your hearts be troubled and do not be afraid" (John 14:1–3, 27). *The world can only give us peace that says, "It probably won't get that bad." Jesus's peace is different. It says, "Even the worst that can happen—your death—is ultimately the best thing that can happen. We all long for a "place" that is truly home. Jesus says that it awaits you.*

Saturday. "If we claim to be without sin, we deceive ourselves and the truth is not in us. If we confess our sins, he is faithful and just and will forgive us our sins and purify us from all unrighteousness. . . . I write this to you so that you will not sin. But if anybody does sin, we have an advocate with the Father—Jesus Christ, the Righteous One" (1 John 1:8–2:1). *If we refuse to admit and try to cover up our sin, God will uncover it. If we will without excuse repent and uncover it, then God will have it covered in the most astonishing way. Believers know that Christ, as it were, stands before the divine bar of justice and is our "advocate" or defense attorney. That is, when God the judge sees us, he sees us "in Christ" and our sins cannot condemn us. Christians have nothing to fear from death or judgment.*

Sunday. "For I consider that the sufferings of this present time are not worth comparing with the glory that is to be revealed to us. . . . What then shall we say to these things? If God is for us, who can be against us? He who did not spare his own Son but gave him up for us all, how will he not also with him graciously give us all things? Who shall bring any charge against God's elect? It is God who justifies. Who is to condemn? Christ Jesus is the one who died—more than that, who was raised—who is at the right hand of God, who indeed is interceding for us. Who shall separate us from the love of Christ? Shall tribulation, or distress, or persecution, or famine, or nakedness, or danger, or sword? . . . No, in all these things we are more than conquerors through him who loved us. For I am sure that neither death nor life, nor angels nor rulers, nor things present nor things to come, nor powers, nor height nor depth, nor anything else in all creation, will be able to separate us from the love of God in Christ Jesus our Lord" (Romans 8:18, 31–35, 37–39 ESV). *The answer to Paul's question is "Nothing! Nothing in Heaven or Earth or anywhere can separate us from the love of God in Christ!" We stand over the coffins of our loved ones, or contemplate our own future death, and are confident that nothing is able to separate us from God.*

If you are facing the death of a loved one

If the death was sudden, don't feel you have to make major life decisions right away, such as where you will live or whether you will change your job. It probably is not a good time to make these decisions. If the loved one has died after a very long illness—or even after a time in which he or she was unconscious or confused—you often begin doing the work of "letting them go" in your heart before they pass away. But if the death comes as an unexpected shock, an air of unreality can cling to you for a good while. It's a sense that you are in a dream or a movie or that you are somebody else. In such a condition, just take it one day at a time, "doing the next thing," not spending too much time with people or too little. As the reality sinks in and you finally begin to let them go, you'll be in a better position to think about your future. But don't do that too quickly.

Be honest about your thoughts and feelings, whether to others, to God, or even to yourself. Don't feel it is "unspiritual" to question and cry out. Remember Jesus weeping and angry at the death of his friend Lazarus. Remember Job crying out to the Lord. Job complained loudly— but he complained to God. He never stopped praying or meeting with God, even though he was not getting much out of it at the time. Just because we know a loved one is with Christ and eventually we will all be together doesn't mean that somehow we should all just be happy now and should stifle our grief and even our anger. Not at all. Jesus didn't stifle his! Nevertheless, don't express emotion in a completely untempered way that would damage you or people around you.

When we have lost a believing loved one, do meditate on the joy he or she has now. When C. S. Lewis's wife died, he heard someone say, "She's in God's hand," and suddenly he got a picture:

> "She is in God's hand." That gains a new energy when I think of her as a sword. Perhaps the earthly life I shared with her was only part of the tempering. Now perhaps He grasps the hilt; weighs the new weapon; makes lightnings with it in the air. "A right Jerusalem

blade." . . . How wicked it would be, if
we could, to call the dead back![2]

If we actually could physically see our loved
ones now, they would be so radiant and beautiful beyond bearing that we would be tempted
to fall down and worship them. Not that they
would let us.

The biggest challenge after losing a loved one
is to realize that the love, joy, and grace that
seem now to be gone are still available, directly from the original source, the Lord himself. There are depths, fountains of power
available in fellowship with Him that you
haven't even tapped. This is not something that
will happen immediately. Don't expect your
prayer life to feel very good now. It will have
the same air of unreality that everything else

does. But eventually, there is comfort and peace available beyond your wildest imagination. When we have other things—spouse, family, friends, health, home, security—we are not driven to really plumb the depths of what is available in communion and prayer. But there are infinite stores of grace. More than enough to get you through the rest of your life—and as a deeper and wiser and even more joyful person (in some ways) than you were before the tragedy. This kind of wound in some ways never goes away. But, like the nail prints in Jesus's hands, they can become "rich wounds . . . in beauty glorified."[3] Have hope that you won't have to always feel as empty as you do now.

Here are some texts to meditate on over the course of a week when facing the death of a loved one. There are seven—one for each day:

Appendix

Monday. "A person's days are determined; you have decreed the number of his months and have set limits he cannot exceed. So look away from him and let him alone till he has put in his time like a hired laborer" (Job 14:5–6). "You have taken from me friend and neighbor—[now] darkness is my closest friend" (Psalm 88:18). *What does it say that God not only allows, even includes, such thoughts in His Word? He knows how we feel and speak when we are desperate.*[4]

Tuesday. "The righteous perish, and no one takes it to heart; the devout are taken away, and no one understands that the righteous are taken away to be spared from evil. Those who walk uprightly enter into peace; they find rest as they lie in death" (Isaiah 57:1, 2). *From our perspective, death—especially for the young—is nothing*

90

but a great evil. Yet we don't know the future, and what if death is God's way of taking people to himself, giving them peace, and saving them from evil. Why is this so counterintuitive for human beings?

Wednesday. Read John 11:17–44. Jesus shows that he sees death from both the perspective of God and from the viewpoint of the bereaved human beings. He weeps with Mary and Martha, yet is moved with anger (verse 38) toward death, even knowing that he will immediately raise Lazarus to life. *Even if God is bringing His people home to Himself, He knows the sorrow and devastation death creates, and grieves with us. Does knowing that God hates death help you in any way?* "Jesus said to her, 'I am the resurrection and the life. The one who believes in me will live, even though they die; and whoever lives by believing in me will never die. Do you believe this?'" (John 11:25–26). *Do you believe this? If you do, how should that affect how you grieve?*

Thursday. "And if Christ has not been raised, your faith is futile; you are still in your sins. Then those also who have fallen asleep in Christ are lost. If only for this life we have hope in Christ, we are of all people most to be pitied. But Christ has indeed been raised from the dead, the firstfruits of those who have fallen asleep. For since death came through a man, the resurrection of the dead comes also through a man. For as in Adam all die, so in Christ all will be made alive" (1 Corinthians 15:17–22). *Paul is staking the credibility of all of Christianity on whether Jesus was raised from the dead or not. If Christian belief is merely a comfort in this life, then we are to be pitied, and those who have died hoping in Christ are gone forever. So before any other of the teaching or claims of Christianity are considered, this is the primary question: Was Jesus raised from the dead? If the answer is yes, then the way forward, though painful, leads to hope. If no, then life is meaningless. Which is it?*

Friday. "For we know that if the earthly tent we live in is destroyed, we have a building from God, an eternal house in heaven, not built by human hands. Meanwhile we groan, longing to be clothed instead with our heavenly dwelling, because when we are clothed, we will not be found naked. For while we are in this tent, we groan and are burdened, because we do not wish to be unclothed but to be clothed instead with our heavenly dwelling, so that what is mortal may be swallowed up by life. Now the one who has fashioned us for this very purpose is God, who has given us the Spirit as a deposit, guaranteeing what is to come" (2 Corinthians 5:1–5). *Paul is specifically rejecting the idea that when we die we become disembodied spirits; instead, we are further clothed, with immortality. This was a theme he had also treated in 1 Corinthians 15, when he talked about the resurrection of the body (verses 42–54). So passing through death is not entering a nebulous, ghostly afterlife, but a life of unimaginable fullness and joy. Our loved ones do not leave us and go into the dark. They leave us and go into the Light.*

Saturday. "The LORD is my shepherd; I shall not want. He makes me lie down in green pastures. He leads me beside still waters. He restores my soul. He leads me in paths of righteousness for his name's sake. Even though I walk through the valley of the shadow of death, I will fear no evil, for you are with me; your rod and your staff, they comfort me. You prepare a table before me in the presence of my enemies; you anoint my head with oil; my cup overflows. Surely goodness and mercy shall follow me all the days of my life and I shall dwell in the house of the LORD forever" (Psalm 23, ESV). *Here is a whole set of comforts for those who grieve. Remember that when you walk into the valley of the shadow of death, it is Jesus, the Shepherd, who has led you there. He has comfort to give you and ways to strengthen, deepen, and grow you that would be otherwise impossible. So give thanks for his presence, refuse self-pity, and seek him in prayer even when you don't feel him present (because he is). Jesus himself walked into* death, solitary and rejected by everyone (Matthew 27:46), so when we face the death of loved ones or even our own death, we will never be alone.

Sunday. "Therefore, there is now no condemnation for those who are in Christ Jesus, because through Christ Jesus the law of the Spirit who gives life has set you free from the law of sin and death" (Romans 8:1–2). *Many people are unaware of the condemnation that has been pronounced over them, or else they are unacquainted with its magnitude, except perhaps for a nagging sense of unease. When facing death, however, our enemy allows us to see the full scope of our cosmic treason, and what answer do we have then? Only this—that Jesus has taken our punishment and set us free, and there is now no condemnation left for us. Rejoice!*

Acknowledgments

As ever, thanks to our editor at Viking, Brian Tart. It was Brian who saw the short meditation on death that I preached at Terry Hall's funeral and proposed that we turn it not only into one but three short books on birth, marriage, and death. We also thank our many friends in South Carolina who made it possible to write this and the companion books while at Folly Beach last summer. Finally and most significantly, I want to thank my wife, Kathy, who did endless iterations of editing to turn my original sermon from the funeral of her sister, Terry Hall, into this short book. Kathy was very much a coauthor. Thanks, honey.

Notes

Foreword

1. From the famous quote by Samuel Johnson, found in James Boswell, *The Life of Samuel Johnson, LLD* (New York: Penguin Classics, 2008), 231.

The Fear of Death: Conscience Makes Cowards of Us All

1. William Shakespeare, *Hamlet*, 4.3.30–31: "A man may fish with the worm that hath eat of a king."
2. Ernest Becker, *The Denial of Death* (New York: The Free Press, 1973), 26.
3. Annie Dillard, *The Living: A Novel* (New York: HarperCollins, 1992), 141.
4. Howard P. Chudacoff, *Children at Play: An American History* (New York: New York University Press, 2007), 22.

5. Atul Gawande, *Being Mortal: Medicine and What Matters in the End* (New York: Metropolitan Books, 2014).

6. Geoffrey Gorer, "The Pornography of Death," 2003. This article may be found at www .romolocapuano.com/wp-content/uploads /2013/08/Gorer.pdf.

7. See David Bosworth, "The New Immortalists," *Hedgehog Review* 17, no. 2 (Summer 2015).

8. Richard A. Shweder, Nancy C. Much, Manamohan Mahapatra, and Lawrence Park, "The 'Big Three' of Morality (Autonomy, Community, Divinity) and the 'Big Three' Explanations of Suffering," in Richard A. Shweder, *Why Do Men Barbecue? Recipes for Cultural Psychology* (Cambridge, MA: Harvard University Press, 2003), 74. For more on this subject, see "The Cultures of Suffering" in Timothy Keller, *Walking with God through Pain and Suffering* (New York: Penguin/ Riverhead, 2013), 13–34.

9. Shweder, *Why Do Men Barbecue? Recipes for Cultural Psychology*, 125.

10. Mark Ashton, *On My Way to Heaven: Facing Death with Christ* (Chorley, UK: 10Publishing, 2010), 7–8.

11. Becker, *The Denial of Death*, xvii.

12. Becker, *The Denial of Death*, xvii.

13. Albert Camus, *The Myth of Sisyphus and Other Essays* (New York: Alfred A. Knopf, 1955).

14. Becker, *The Denial of Death*, 26–27.

15. See Julian Barnes, *Nothing to Be Frightened Of* (London: Jonathan Cape, 2008). The article by Jessica E. Brown, "We Fear Death, but What If Dying Isn't as Bad as We Think?," is from *The Guardian*, July 25, 2017.

16. Luc Ferry, *A Brief History of Thought: A Philosophical Guide to Living* (New York: Harper, 2010), 4.

17. From Dylan Thomas, *In Country Sleep, and Other Poems* (London: Dent, 1952). The poem can be found at www.poets.org/poetsorg /poem/do-not-go-gentle-good-night.

18. Quoted in Wilfred M. McClay, "The Strange Persistence of Guilt," *Hedgehog Review* 19, no. 1 (Spring 2017).

19. McClay, "The Strange Persistence of Guilt."

20. McClay, "The Strange Persistence of Guilt."

21. Andrew Delbanco, *The Death of Satan: How Americans Have Lost the Sense of Evil* (New York: Farrar, Straus and Giroux, 1995), 3, 9.

22. David Brooks, "The Cruelty of Call-Out Culture," *New York Times*, January 14, 2019.

23. McClay, "The Strange Persistence of Guilt."

24. From Eliot, "Murder in the Cathedral," in *The Complete Plays of T. S. Eliot* (New York: Harcourt, Brace, and World, Inc., 1935), 43.

25. *Hamlet*, 3.1.87–88, 91.

26. This story was related by Dr. Leitch to a group of college students, of which I was one, at Bucknell University in 1970.

27. William L. Lane, Word Biblical Commentary *Hebrews 1–8,* vol. 47, (Dallas, TX: Word Books, 1991), 55–58.

28. C. S. Lewis, "The Weight of Glory," is found at www.newcityindy.org/wp-content/uploads/2012/06/Lewis-Weight-of-Glory.pdf.

29. Margaret N. Barnhouse, *That Man Barnhouse* (Carol Stream, IL: Tyndale House, 1983), 186.

The Rupture of Death:
Do Not Grieve Like Those Without Hope

1. See any commentary. One example: George R. Beasley-Murray, *John*, vol. 36, Word Biblical Commentary (Plano, TX: Thomas Nelson, 1999), 194.

2. Homer, *The Iliad*, 24.549–51, quoted in N. T.

Wright, *The Resurrection of the Son of God* (Minneapolis, MN: Fortress Press, 2003), 2.

3. Peter Kreeft, *Love Is Stronger Than Death* (San Francisco: Ignatius Press, 1979), 2–3.

4. See Jonathan Edwards, "Sermon Fifteen: Heaven Is a World of Love," in *The Works of Jonathan Edwards*, WJE Online, Jonathan Edwards Center, Yale University, edwards .yale.edu/archive?path=aHR0cDovL2Vkd2Fy ZHMueWFsZS5lZHUvY2dpLWJpbi9uZXkd waGlssby9nZXRvYmplY3QucGw/Yy43O jQ6MTUud2plbw==.

5. From the hymn "Sometimes a Light Surprises," William Cowper, 1779.

6. C. S. Lewis, "The Weight of Glory," is found at www.newcityindy.org/wp-content/uploads /2012/06/Lewis-Weight-of-Glory.pdf.

7. John Flavel, *Pneumatologia: A Treatise of the Soul of Man.* In *The Works of John Flavel*, vol. 3 (Edinburgh: Banner of Truth Trust, 1968), 121. Some of the language is modernized.

8. Cited in F. F. Bruce, *1 and 2 Thessalonians*, vol. 45, Word Biblical Commentary (Plano, TX: Thomas Nelson, 1982), 96.

9. For example, see N. T. Wright, *Resurrection of the Son of God*, 32–206.

10. C. S. Lewis, *Mere Christianity* (New York: Macmillan, 1960), 174–75.

Appendix

1. From "How Firm a Foundation," a hymn by John Rippon, 1787.
2. C. S. Lewis, *A Grief Observed* (New York: HarperOne, 2001), 63, 76.
3. From "Crown Him with Many Crowns," a hymn by Matthew Bridges and Godfrey Thring, 1851.
4. Derek Kidner, *Psalms 1–72: An Introduction and Commentary* (Leicester, UK: Inter-Varsity Press, 1973), 157.

Further Reading

Joseph Bayly. *The View from a Hearse*. Elgin, IL.: David C. Cook, 1969.

Elisabeth Elliot. *Facing the Death of Someone You Love*. Westchester, IL.: Good News Publishers, 1982.

Timothy Keller. *Walking with God Through Pain and Suffering*. New York: Penguin/Riverhead, 2013.

Timothy Keller. *Making Sense of God: Finding God in the Modern World*. New York: Penguin, 2016.

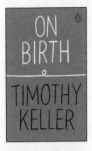
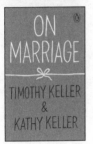